A Discoverie of Witches

A Discoverie of Witches

BLAKE MORRISON

Litfest
&
Smith / Doorstop

Litfest
The Storey
Meeting House Lane
Lancaster LA1 1TH
Company Registered in England and Wales no. 1494221
Registered Charity no. 510670

and

Smith/Doorstop Books
an imprint of The Poetry Business
Bank Street Arts
32-40 Bank Street
Sheffield S1 2DS
Company Registered in England and Wales no. 02644139

Litfest
ISBN 978-0-9540880-5-7 ePub
ISBN 978-0-9540880-8-8 Hardback
ISBN 978-0-9540880-7-1 Limited Edition

Smith / Doorstop
ISBN 978-1-906613-60-0 Hardback

FSC

Copyright © Blake Morrison 2012

The right of Blake Morrison to be identified as the author of this work has been asserted by him in accordance with the Copyright, Designs and Patents Act, 1988.

All rights reserved. No part of this publication may be reproduced, stored in or introduced into a retrieval system, or transmitted, in any form, or by any means (electronic, mechanical, photocopying, recording or otherwise) without the prior written permission of the publisher. Any person who does any unauthorised act in relation to this publication may be liable to criminal prosecution and civil claims for damages.

Cover design by Gareth Dennison.

Litfest wish to thank Lancaster County Council and Lancashire County Council.
The Poetry Business gratefully acknowledges the help of Arts Council England.

To Karl

Preface

IN AUGUST 1612 A SERIES OF WITCHCRAFT TRIALS TOOK PLACE AT LANCASTER ASSIZES. Over twenty men and women from the Pendle area of Lancashire were charged with a variety of offences, ranging from murder and cannibalism to the causing of sickness through witchcraft. Ten of the accused were found guilty and hanged, the majority of them after confessing to their crimes. Many similar trials took place in Britain, Europe and America before 1612 and after, but the Pendle witch trials became famous partly because of the number of those involved and partly because the clerk of the court, Thomas Potts, published a detailed account of the proceedings. The Pendle witches soon became part of folklore and they remain famous to this day – a tourist industry flourishes around them. When I was growing up on the Lancashire-Yorkshire border, with Pendle Hill visible in the distance, talk of witches was commonplace; every local village seemed to have one – or rather, every village had an old woman whose behaviour and appearance struck fear into the hearts of children. What had happened in 1612 seemed close in time. Our village still had a wooden stocks and it was easy to imagine witches being placed in them. Sorcery and spookiness weren't reserved for Hallowe'en.

Hannah Arendt spoke of the 'banality of evil', and in the context of the Pendle witches the phrase is apt. What began as a commonplace feud between two families rose to a pitch of hysteria, with every illness or death throughout the area, whether of humans or animals, attributed to the malevolence of witches. Accusations flew back and forth. And when a pedlar complained that a woman called Alizon Device had paralysed him after he refused to sell her pins, a local magistrate intervened. The trials themselves were extraordinary for reasons that resonate to this day: because child witnesses were allowed to give evidence; because those accused confessed to crimes which they could not possibly have committed; and because the sentences imposed were so harsh. Four hundred years on, we like to think we handle things better. But our judicial system is still flawed. And suspicion of and hostility towards the Other persist to this day; it's only the names of the scapegoats that have changed. A few years ago, when the British National Party was making gains in the Pendle area, I interviewed one of their candidates in Nelson. His grudge was against immigrants and their alien ways. I couldn't help noticing he had books about witchcraft on his shelves.

The Pendle witches don't conform either to Harry Potter stereotypes or to the image constructed in *Macbeth*, which was written six years before the Lancaster trials. Spells are cast and clay images pricked with pins. But there are no broomsticks, no steaming cauldrons and no witches' Sabbaths. Satan has a role to play but he appears in the guise of a dog or hare, not as a devil with horns. And there's nothing especially spine-chilling about the motives for witchcraft. It happens when someone behaves meanly or intemperately and has a curse put on them in return. Grudges, superstition, a belief in charms and otherworldly spirits: all this seems perfectly familiar. The witches may look ugly but they're also homely – the dysfunctional neighbours across the street.

Several of the poems in this book were prompted less by the Pendle witch trials than by the Pennine landscapes I lived among as a child. Bleak moors, rain and wind sweeping over heather, godforsaken spots it feels scary to be in after dusk – this is the territory of witches. But it's also home, my place of origin, and these are the landscapes I carry round in my head. They're dark but also beautiful landscapes, disquieting but uplifting. That's the quality I look for in writing as well.

In 1996, the artist Paula Rego illustrated nine of my poems for a book entitled *Pendle Witches*, after one of the poems. For this collection, I've revised the contents so as to focus more closely on Pendle and the Pennines; only four poems from the earlier book are included, but several from my *Selected Poems* of 1999 have been added. Among them is 'The Ballad of the Yorkshire Ripper', which takes as its theme male fear and hatred of women – a theme pertinent to the demonising of witches. I've also added a number of new poems which in one way or another draw on motifs from witchcraft, including 'Crizum Child' (which was inspired by a prayer taught to one of the child witnesses at the Lancaster trials), 'Besom', 'The Mark', 'Corinne and the Witches' (a reworking of one of Ovid's *Amores*), and, by far the longest, 'A Discoverie of Witches' (the title drawn from Thomas Potts's book of 1612, *The Wonderfull Discoverie of Witches in the Countie of Lancaster*), which weaves a prose narrative loosely based on the Pendle witch trials with poems, quotes from contemporary documents, squibs, nursery rhymes and nonsense verse.

Blake Morrison
March, 2012

Some of these poems appeared previously in *Dark Glasses* (Chatto, 1984), *The Ballad of the Yorkshire Ripper* (Chatto, 1987), *Pendle Witches* (Enitharmon, 1996), and *Selected Poems* (Granta, 1999).

Contents

Preface ... VII

Part One

Pendle Witches ... 15
Crizum Child ... 16
The Mark ... 17
Corrine and the Witches ... 18
Old Witches ... 20
Thumb ... 21
Besom ... 22
A Discoverie of Witches ... 23

Part Two

Pomagne ... 43
Whinny Moor ... 44
Grange Boy ... 47
Metamorphoses of Childhood ... 49
A Provincial Fiction ... 52
Back ... 53
Shed Load ... 54
Cuckoo-pint ... 55
Isabella's Song ... 56
Meningococcus ... 57
Up on the Hill ... 58
Gisburne Park ... 60

Part Three

The Ballad of the Yorkshire Ripper ... 65

When I consider whether there are such persons as witches, my mind is divided: I believe, in general, that there is such a thing as witchcraft, but can give no credit to any particular instance of it.

Joseph Addison

Part One

Pendle Witches

On recs and at swimming pools
we searched for the girl
shy and uncomeatable –
through whose glimming thigh-tops

the light would make a perfect O,
that florin emptiness
not the token of a virgin
but the hole in a lemmel-stone

to ward off the hags
who ran the Pennines
and who wanted to trap us
in the sossy peat of their maw.

Crizum Child

What is that light on Pendle Hill breaking so farrandly?
It is my Crizum child nailed high upon a tree.

I fed him wheat-baps when we rose just after daybreak,
and frumenty and buttermilk and Chorley cake,
then he went from me to the scule-house for his Latin
but from the hedge a nest of hell-hags crept and grabbed him
and hauled him up the hillside to the rowan
and pinned him high and spread him wide with rusty iron.

We have sent out for the carpenter in Salterforth
but he's away and won't be back until the sabbath
and with the blood streaming down my poor child's body
I fear he'll never be unfastened from that rood-tree
for though I've prayed to God to spare my only Crizum
it seems that God prefers to keep him in his prison.

Well, if he dies then I will take me to the coven
where the crones sit boiling mischief in their stew-pan,
and I will cleave their bones and skulltops with my sickle
till I've silenced every spell and hiss and cackle,
then I'll go unto that light that breaks so farrandly
and be at peace on Pendle Hill at last, my child and me.

The Mark

Depending how you looked at it
the bruise on her neck
as she stood at the altar
was the stamp of the Devil
or the bite her lover left
the night of her last fling.

'Does anyone know…?' But no one did.
Pressing his mouth to it,
her husband felt his lips burn
and swore it tasted of damson.

Corinne and the Witches
after Ovid

This old hag undertook to suborn our relationship,
And a glibly poisonous tongue she had for the job.
                                    Amores, Book 1, Poem 8

The problem wasn't Corinne but her friends: the witches, I called them.
Not that they wore black, rode brooms or made stews
flavoured with herbs and magic potions, but they had power –
the power to turn her against me.
We'd be getting on fine, never better, till an evening down the wine bar
would poison things. I wasn't there to hear
exactly what those hellhags said but from her coldness
towards me afterwards I knew.
'See the man at the bar staring at you? The one in the Armani suit?
Go for it, girl. What's holding you back?
With looks like yours you should be living in a penthouse, not a garret.
Being faithful's well and good, but the bard
you're shacked up with isn't worth it. Take your chances while you can.
None of us is getting any younger.
Looks are like brass: without attention they lose their lustre.
Admiring glances make a woman glow.
You're guileless, that's your problem. The money you could be spending
on clothes you waste on him and his rotten odes.
Refuse to give your body to him till he gives you something in return.
Sulk, throw a tantrum, use an onion:
if tears don't bring him into line, nothing will. And don't let him think
he's the only dolphin in your ocean.
Rumple the sheets on your bed before he gets home.
Pinch your skin to make a bruise or two.
Put the phone down quickly when he walks into the room.
Tricks like these will drive him nuts.

And don't go feeling guilty about it. Suffering's good for poets.
- sweetie, it's your *duty* to hurt him.
If the worst happens and you dump him (God knows, we wouldn't blame you),
you can be sure he'll get a sonnet from it.
That's what muses are for: to drive their lovers to distraction.
Make him miserable and he will make art.'
Art? Verses anyway. Here I am in my garret laying a curse
on the crones who weaned my Corinne from me.
While she lies in the arms of her new lover, they cackle in the wine bar
and I spit green-flecked poison onto the page.

Old Witches

The more blind, deaf, lame, arthritic,
hairy-chinned, bowbacked and incontinent,
the greater the power they have.

Their bony hands encircle your wrist,
their lips issue instructions,
Light the oven, let the cat in, sweep the floor,

Fetch that box of potions from my dresser,
and you do, how can you not,
till the day your patience runs out.

Once they were hanged or drowned.
Today it's more subtle:
a pillow when no one's looking

or an overdose of morphine
- a kindness to them as well as to you.

Thumb

Here I have a pilot's thumb,
Wrecked as homeward he did come.
                    Macbeth, Act 1, Scene 3: First Witch

What a thrill,
his thumb like a dildo,
the nifty knuckle
working away

at the hidden thing -
press stud, bell push,
flesh-button sewn
in folds of flesh -

and the moon
of his cuticle
carrying me upwards
through the sky.

Cries in the night.
An answered bell.
Dirty girl.
Thumb stump.

Besom

As well as the witches who made crops fail,
heifers drop dead, troublesome neighbours
take to their bed and never get up again,

there was one whose potions made the blood sing,
so when she took you under her wing
what you found wasn't a broom of thwacky twigs

but a brush so soft and satin that to ride it
was ecstatic and led you to fresh meadows
and the rushing silver waters of a weir.

A Discoverie of Witches

In Pendle at that time were found all the most arrant sorcerers, inchanters, veneficks, maleficks, wizards and witches in the kingdom. Even the best of men trembled to cross them, lest he pay for it with his life.

～

And one there lived that by common fame was accompted a witch.
When she hiccocked, wrens flew out of her mouth.
And when she sneezed, bees swarmed from her nose.
Many a kitling died from her spells.
Many a wether was afflicted with tisick.
And it was bruited her daughter and grand-daughter were witches too,
she having taught them the malefic arts.

～

Fence, Sabden, Blacko and Colne:
Home to a coven of whiskered crones.
Colne, Blacko, Sabden and Fence:
Home to black magic and frankincense.

The Trough of Bowland and Pendle Hill:
A curse from a witch and your child falls ill.
The Hill of Pendle and Bowland Trough:
A curse from a witch and your milk goes off.

A portion of Lancs, just over from Yorks:
Land of mad hell-hags with claws like hawks.
Just over from Yorks, a portion of Lancs:
Land of viragos and mountebanks.

～

The happenings of that time were like a butter-pat leaving ridges on butter – all who lived there were marked by them.

The trouble commenced many years past when one called Demdike (then a young wench) went to cross the Ribble at Samlesbury by boat. On the riverbank she met the devil in the shape of a brown dog that promised if she let him suck on some secret part of her she would be granted the power to do anything on this earth, whereupon she was enticed, and let him suck blood from under her arm.

Then another time this brown dog did meet her on the byway and carried her into a barn and laid her on the floor and covered her with straw then himself lay on top of the straw till her speech and senses were taken from her, and the next she knew she was at home in her bed.

And another time as the sun fell at daygate he came as a hare that stood on its hind legs and took her to the barn again and did lie with her on top of a haymow, and got blood from her flesh, she being without apparel save for a smock, and the hare being no hare but a malkin.

Now this Demdike in those days was reckoned a healer, whom many would call on when they were afflicted and who for the privilege of her arts would in return demand coins or bread. But in time folk lost faith in her, since those she laid hands on rarely recovered, nor their cattle neither, and when she parted from them she sang this mocking song:

Your loaf in my lap,
Your penny in my purse.
You're never the better
And I'm never the worse.

Came the day when none employed her again, and she grew bitter and let the devil lie with her every night and became a witch in earnest.

∽

The people there are given to little or no kind of labour, living very hardy with oaten bread, sour whey and goats' milk, dwelling far from any church or chapel, and are as ignorant of God or any civil course of life as the very savages amongst the infidels.

⁓

Hickory, dickory dock.
The mouse ran up the clock.
The clock struck one
A witch flew down
Trickery, tickery, tock.

⁓

And Demdike had a daughter called Elizabeth, who was deformed about the face, with the left eye looking down at the hearth while the right looked up the chimney. One day there came to her a thing in the likeness of a spotted bitch that offered her butter, cheese and a half-stone of oatmeal yearly for all time. The temptation of such riches was too strong, and she joined her mother in spreading wickedness.

The way they practised witchcraft was to make mommets – that is a picture out of clay like unto the person whom they meant to harm. And when they would have the person be ill in any one place more than another, then they took a thorn or pin and pricked it in that part of the picture. And when they would have any part of the body to consume away, they took that part of the picture and burned it. And when they would have the person die, they took the whole of the picture and cast it in the fire.

⁓

'Hibble-hubble, toil and trouble.
Hair of vole and squirrel stubble.
Stir the broth and watch it bubble.
Double-double toil and trouble.

'Worse and worser, bad and badder
Eye of newt and skin of adder,
Cockroach crunch and beetle bladder,
Swill them round and drive folks madder.'

Fiddle-faddle, scribble-scrabble
Hear the witches as they gabble,
Cooking up their psychic babble,
That rabid, rat-faced Ribble rabble.

∼

Why are so many witches women?
 First they are by nature credulous, wanting experience and therefore more easily deceived.
 Second they harbour in their breasts a curious desire to know such things as be not fitting and convenient.
 Third, their minds are softer, and thus more easily receive the impressions of the devil.
 Fourth, in them is the greater facility to fall, as was first shown by Eve.
 Fifth, this sex, when it conceiveth wrath or hatred against any, is unplacable, and possessed with unsatiable desire of revenge.
 Sixth, women are of slippery tongue and full of words, and being unable to keep knowledge of wicked practices to themselves thereby disperse them.

∼

As mother and daughter plotted together, so their influence became more malign.
 One who was bewitched, Isabel, vomited pins.
 Another, Jane, was riddling flour through her sieve when a hedgepig leapt out and blinded her.
 Also bewitched was Ursula, who on Hallowmass, about four of the afternoon, went to her master's house, having nine beasts to milk, and while pulling at the teats she felt a prick in her side, and the cow likewise started

with pain and kicked the pail over. And going homewards with a piggin full of milk, still stricken above the heart, she espied by the stile a large black dog that stared back at her, this being the last she saw before falling senseless and later having to be helped home in a chair.

And this dog she had suspicion of being the spirit that served Alizon, daughter to Elizabeth, whom she had offended by not giving her some curds she coveted.

For Alizon was heard whistling the dog to her side from under a crabtree and she fed it milk and let it lie in the wool she had by her for spinning. And this same Alizon was said to keep imps in an earthen pot and to feed them from a spoon.

Now the people of Pendle drew together and muttered complaints. The rancid butter they churned, the beer they brewed that stank and had to be put in the swill tub, the goslings that died together at three month, the blood instead of milk that streamed from the goat, the lamb with its neck awry, the wind that ruined the barley, the plums that rotted, the spindle that glowed hot and snapped the thread, the horses that went lame after drinking from the weir – were not all these the doings of witches?

No smoke without fire.
No sickness without poison.
No deaths without a witch.

If a witch has turned your milk sour, then plunge a red-hot horse-shoe in the churn and the milk will taste sweet again.

If a witch has been haunting your house, then take a piece of white paper and write on it in green ink 'God bless me here in time, and there eternally', and place this on your bedstead.

If a witch has made your children ill, then mix their urine with grain to bake a cake and have them eat it.

If a witch has made your cattle run wild, then stop her in the road and scratch her face to draw blood and smear the blood about the hide of your beasts, and they will be placid again.

And if a witch has bewitched you, take hog's dung and charvel, hold them in your left hand, and then with a knife in the other hand prick them three times, and cast them in the fire, and put six leaves of sage in a mug of ale and drink of it, and then next day you will be cured.

~

Tickery, trickery tock
The hour-hand on the clock
Became a man
With a watering-can
And a dickery, wickery cock.

~

Now more than these three witches lived in Pendle. There was also Chattox – a withered, spent, decrepit creature, her lips ever chattering, whose sight had almost gone - and her daughter Anne. This Anne as a maid was so comely that the man on whose land she bided, Robert Nutter, demanded his pleasure of her and when she denied him called her whore. When Anne told her mother this, Chattox hissed like a branding-iron in water, and set about plaguing him, and shortly afterwards he died.

In time even goodly people befriended these witches, so as to come to no harm - or else to use their services.

One was Ellen, who wanted revenge on William the shoemaker after he charged her two groats for new laces.

Another was Alice, a woman of wealth who had little to gain from abetting these poor beggars, but who did it for the pleasure of sinning.

Three young cousins of the witches also joined the mischief for want of better things to do.

And two men, John and James, discovered that when witches sup ale any man can have his pleasure with them, so they brought barrels and fiddles and hung about their skirts.

'Something must be done to stop this wickedness,' said the priest from his pulpit in Gisburn.

Ugliness is one sign.
If her eyes are sunk in her head
or there are warts on her back,
she's in league with Satan.

But a lass past forty who's slim
with milky-white skin
and no wrinkles
has also sold her soul to him.

And any muttering pieties
about witchcraft having no power
now she's put her trust in God
is a hellcat in disguise.

For proof, we duck them in a beck.
The innocent drown.
Women who float are rescued
then strung up by the neck.

Our Lord and Master King James has writ that there are two ways to tell a witch: by finding her mark – the devil's mark – and watching if she stays numb when it is pricked; or the swimming test, whereby her left toe is roped to her right thumb, and vice versa, and she thrown in a mill dam and left to drown - if guilty she will bob there happy as an apple.

They were rebels that wore black clothes
And made loud music after sunset
And threw their bones unwashed in the midden
And who if you knocked at their door to ask
Would they be more neighbourly
Would glower and set their dogs on you.
And this was why we summoned the magistrate.
For rebellion is as the sin of witchcraft
And thou shalt not suffer a witch to live.

∿

These credulous folk make witches into gods. But if all the witches in England were burnt or hanged, I warrant you we should not fail to have rain, hail and tempests as we have now. For such come by the appointment and will of God.

∿

There are three ways toothless women can bite:
With an evil eye, wicked tongue or icy heart.
But if they do, then the biters will be bit
And perish in the teeth of bitter hate.

∿

The way the witches were caught was this, that one day Alizon, granddaughter to Demdike, was too frank in casting a spell. A pedlar called Law would not give her some pins she asked for, so she used her spirit, a black dog, to strike him senseless. When he recovered his speech and reported this, a magistrate was sent for, one Roger Nowell, a very religious honest gentleman, who made enquiries throughout Pendle and Craven.

 Demdike swore that Chattox was a witch.
 Chattox swore that Demdike was a witch.
 Alizon swore she was herself a witch, since having let the Devil suck of her breast a little below the paps, which remained blue for half a year thereafter.

Alizon's brother James swore that Chattox had once dug up some skulls and taken eight teeth from them, and given half to Demdike, so each could do mischief.

In consequence, Master Nowell sent Demdike and her grand-daughter Alizon to the dungeon in Lancaster to await trial, and Chattox and her daughter Anne also.

Other witches were questioned but swore they did no harm and that their neighbours had slandered them.

～

Their wives are gossips who spy on us.
Their children make up lies about us.
Their dogs are trained to chase us away.
But our herbs are used to heal –
vervain the skin, hyssop the head, mugwort the heart -
and our spells to make the village prosper:
so bread rises higher in the oven,
and milk flows freer from cows' teats,
and pigs grow fatter in the byre.

～

They have so frayed us with spirits, elves, hags, fairies, satyrs, pans, fauns, dwarfs, giants, imps, changelings, hobgoblins and other such bugs that we are afraid of our own shadows.

～

Gunpowder, treason and plot,
A scheme brewed in the pot
To cross the Dales,
Blow up the jail
And free all the crones on the spot.

～

On Good Friday, Demdike's daughter Elizabeth summoned friends of the prisoners to meet together at Malkin Tower. The wind blew bitter cold, but they merrily roasted a sheep, and drank wine, and blasphemed against our Lord on the day of His crucifixion, and toasted Guy Fawkes for his plot with gunpowder some years before, and resolved to outperform him by blowing up Lancaster Castle, and murdering the gaoler, and setting free the women entombed there.

When word of this scheme got out, the conspirators were caught and put in the dungeon, apart from a few that fled.

While they were held there in the darkness, one they knew well from Gisburn, Jennet Preston, was hanged in York for having murdered her master four years before, the proof of it lying in this, that when she touched his corpse fresh blood flowed from it.

Meanwhile old Demdike died in that dungeon from lack or water and fresh straw.

It will have blood, they say; blood will have blood.
Snails have been known to run and trees to speak,
And the stones that witches wear about their neck
Can conjure doves to eat the eggs of their own brood.

It must have blood, they say, men must have blood.
For ease they turn on those with blood that leaks,
And beat them like a mallet tendering steaks,
And so the days grow darker and more cold.

Be it enacted by the King our sovereign that if any person or persons shall exercise any invocation or conjuration of evil spirits; or shall consult, covenant with, entertain, employ, feed or reward any wicked spirit for some intent or purpose; or take up any dead man, woman or child out of his, her or their grave; or employ any part of the dead person in the manner of sorcery, charm or enchantment; or shall practise witchcraft whereby a person is killed, wasted, consumed, pained or lamed in his or her body: that any such offender or offenders, and their aiders, abetters and counsellors, being lawfully convicted, shall suffer pain of death as a felon or felons, and shall lose the benefit of clergy and sanctuary.

'The darkest corner of the realm', they say.
But we're used to darkness, on the Northern Circuit,
And the case that began in the Assizes that day
Had nothing new or eerie-strange to it.
I had dealt with witches already, in York.
Feuding families, peasant ignorance, village
Idiots abusing each other – this was my kind of work.
Only the numbers surprised me, because so large,
Over a dozen facing the gallows.
My face stayed grave as I heard the evidence.
Though some were simpletons and others scallies,
to all that spoke I listened with patience.
My good name was at stake; the court's as well.
The scales of justice had to look level.

Perhaps, possibly, might, may:
Live again another day.
Likely, probably, surely, must:
Ashes to ashes, dust to dust.

In the trials of that time, in Lancashire and beyond, many a witness came forth to denounce witches.

   One woman while washing clothes had thrown a little water out the window, some of which fell on a witch that happened to be passing. Soon after the cradle in which woman had laid her baby was thrown over, shattered to pieces and the child fell down and was killed.

Another saw a rat scut up the chimney and fall down again in the likeness of a toad, at which the witch, taking it up with tongs, thrust it in the fire and held it till the flames burned blue, but when the toad was released it was uncharred and hopped away.

And one man carrying thatch for his roof had his cart halted outside a cottage, and though the ground there was flat and stony he could not move the cart back or forward for an hour or more, and this was proof that the cottage was a witch's cottage.

And an honest farmer that loved the pot told how he had been drinking in a tavern with four malt-worms like himself when in walked a woman whom he jolly greeted with 'Look, boys, a witch, you can tell it by her cankered nose.' The witch stood there in a chafe, staring pins at him, till he stepped outside in the alley to piss, and drew out his gentleman usher, which he found to be cankered, like the witch's nose. That night it grew more cankered still and in the morrow it fell off.

～

You expect a judge to credit a tale like that?
I am saying only what happened.
You are certain she is a witch?
All who know her believe she is.
If you believe a thing does that make it so?
Because I crossed her, she made the Devil haunt me.
Does not the Devil haunt all men continually?
I suffered with griping belly pains.
What if the pains came by natural causes?
The woman admits she has satanick powers.
Might not she be deluded?
She has told how the devil possessed her.
If under his command, is she to blame?
I cannot sleep safe while she lives.
Is not death too harsh a punishment?

She has made me poor by killing all my cattle.
Do you not still have a dozen healthy cows?
I keep them safe from her by lifting up their tails and kissing beneath.
I say you are too far in love with your cows.

⁓

A witch in time goes centuries back.
A witch in rhyme has a pointed hat.
A witch in quick-lime will not survive.
A witch in St Ives has umpteen lives.
A witch in the fire will save on logs.
A witch in the byre will poison hogs.
A Lancashire witch is fine once dead.
Better hanged than living in your head.

⁓

Some who testified at the trials were not yet fully grown.

Jennet, just nine, spoke against her mother Elizabeth, who ranted at her so fearfully that the child shed tears and her mother was led from court. Then they stood Jennet on a table and bade her continue and she recounted all the murthers her mother had done by using spirits.

Grace, fourteen, narrated the worst depravity of all, when two women fetched a baby from its cot, and thrust a nail into its navel and then a straw through which they whistled a merry tune. The child did not cry out at being hurt but later it languished and died, after which they put it in a pot to broil on the coals, and ate the flesh thereof and gnawed the bones and anointed themselves with the fat.

And Grace swore this to be true, saying the women had cajoled her to join with them in the mischief but that she had refused. Likewise when they with another woman took her to the banks of the Ribble to dance and swyve with four black demons disguised as men, she would not let her body be abused, but kept her smock firm around her knees.

The women stood to die because of Grace's story but then it came out that it had been fed to her by a priest and they were acquitted. But Jennet was believed and her mother sentenced to die.

∼

I've nothing to tell.
Isobel
bewitched me with a spell.

I stole the baby.
Ruby
put the stake through its heart, not me.

I put it in the vat.
Pat
said let's boil it for its fat.

I'm not an animal.
Annabel
made me play at being a cannibal.

I gnawed one bone.
Joan
chopped the gristle up to make scones.

I buried the remains.
Jane
dug them up and sucked out the brains.

I repented my sin.
Lynn
cavorted with a wicked grin.

I do confess
I did some mischief, yes,
But it were nowt to what was done by all the rest.

How was it that the Devil and you first met?
He appeared to me at dead of night.
What shape did he appear in when he spoke?
The shape of a sheepdog, white and black.
Did he say what was the purpose of his call?
He asked would I surrender him my soul.
And what did you speak in reply to this?
I stared him in the eye and answered yes.
Were you not held in fearsome terror of him?
At first I was – but then he sucked and I felt calm.
In what place did he suck to make you content?
A place of his choosing, above the fundament.
How long would he continue to suck there?
Upwards of an hour, till he could suck no more.
Did you ever feel or touch the Devil?
I stroked his back, at which he wagged his tail.
What words did he speak when the sucking was over?
He asked what could he give me for the favour.
So what things did you ask him in return?
To suffer cattle to sicken and hayricks to burn.
Did you not bid him further harms than those?
I asked him to acquit me some revenges.
For men and women to be made to die?
Just a few whom I counted as my enemy.
Why until now did you forswear all this?
Shame and sorrow made me hide it in lies.
And now you wish to seek atonement with the truth?
Not to save my life, but the better to face death.
So you repent all your mischief and your evil?

All but letting myself be sucked by the Devil.
You still take pleasure in that iniquity?
I loved to feel his lips against my body.
You say this fully knowing you may die?
Without him I feel dead already.
Hereby concludes our examination.
What is the verdict of the jury, foreman?
'That she being guilty no mercy be shown.'
Then take her straight to the gallows. Amen

~

It is a principle of the law of nature that any enemie to the state should be put to death; now the most notorious traytor and rebel that can be is the witch.

~

I served my country well, or the jury
Did, at my direction: ten hanged, five acquitted,
One ordered to stand in the pillory.
I've not been officially congratulated
But I'm told the king has heard the story
And a promotion to the south is guaranteed.
A happy outcome then. If I've some pity
For the women that were executed,
I also feel scorn at their gullibility.
There were crimes they could not have committed
Yet they confessed to them repeatedly
Even without being tortured and tried.
Why let their deaths make me feel guilty?
Notoriety was what they wanted.
Thanks to me, they will have it for eternity.

~

The hangings were just, for what witches had ever made such liberal and voluntary confessions of their meetings, plots, offences, bloody practices and what not? The evidence against them was weighty but their own testimony exceeded it, and their skill in convicting themselves betrayed an eagerness to have done with their lives. Even more might have been hanged, for as the judge said to those acquitted, 'although it pleased God out of his mercy to spare you at this time, yet without question there are among you some that are as deep in this action as any of them condemned to die.'

Sorcery, mischief and plot,
The witches warmed the pot.
A toad plopped in
A judge stepped out
And cut off the heads of the lot.

Less zeal would have been the overture of revolution. If those women had been acquitted, the country people would have been encouraged to trespass in even greater degree and some disorder or havoc been committed that troubled the whole realm.

It were enough to crack an hangman's heart.
Old, ragged, with chains about their ankles,
they were fetched to where I waited on the hill,
hissed and spat at by the sweating mob
and convinced to the end - the end of a rope -
that the power they stood accused of
were a power they truly possessed.

Each crossed herself as she climbed the steps
and none cried out as I tied the noose.
Witches? These were not witches,
only weak and half-cracked biddies
undone by wicked gossip and revenge.
It were enough to crack an hangman's heart
but not - I'm pleased to tell you, sire - the rope.

～

And when they examined Elizabeth's body, they found in her private parts a mark of which they'd never seen the like. It was the devil's mark, in the proportions of a small grape or berry and shaped somewhat like a teat. And this was proof she had been justly hanged.

But several lamented Alizon's death who before had been her utter enemies, and wished she were alive. Their penitence was touching, but she would have been the more beholden to them had they kept her from the gallows rather than cutting the rope after she was hanged.

With the witches gone, peace slowly returned to the land and few who lived there ever thought of them again - though from time to time since, in the same county of Lancashire, a strange music has been heard that drives the people to frenzy.

～

And when they appeared with their long black hair
Out of the cavern and struck up their sounds
We were possessed by the strangest yearning
And shook our heads and trembled through our veins
And could not help but scream our hearts out.
Oh Mersey, we cried, have Mersey on us,
And let the music pour out forever.

Part Two

Pomagne

'Be careful not to spill it when it pops.
They'd bloody crucify me if they caught us.'

We had taken months to get to this,
our first kiss a meeting of stalagmite

and stalactite. The slow drip of courtship:
her friend, June, interceding with letters,

the intimate struggle each Friday
under the Plaza's girder of light.

But here we were at last, drinking Pomagne
in her parents' double bed, Christmas Eve

and the last advent-calendar door.
'Did you hear the gate click?' 'No, did you?'

Whinny Moor

*Old people will tell you that after death the soul passes over
Whinny-moore, a place full of whins and brambles, and…would be met
by an old man carrying a huge bundle of boots; and if among these could
be found a pair which the bare-footed soul had given away during life,
the old man gave them to the soul to protect its feet whilst crossing the
thorny moor.*

I was back walking on Lothersdale Moor,
through ling, blackthorn and blips of sheepshit,
over dry-stone walls and up kestrels' airstreams,
back with the becks and original sources,
to land on the fell road under Pinhaw
beside the steamed-up hatchback of a Ford.

The driver's window opened as I stood there.
'Tha'll catch thi death – get in an warm thisen,'
said the heathery face, open, bloodshot,
leaning across to unlock the other door.
I limped around and took my seat beside him,
cupping my bones about his leather flask.

That highland nip restored me to the land
of the living and I warmed to my tale:
how I had hiked the backs of the Pennine Way,
leaving at dawn from Todmorden to end –
'down there, see, if this mist would just clear up
a bit' – in the shade of Thornton Church.

He glanced, disbelieving, at my plimsolls,
frayed and holy with a flapping sole.
He was a rep for Peter Lord, he said,
nodding behind him at the bootful of boots.
'Ah've worked in shoes near alf a century
an sin all t'flippin lot go reet down'ill.'

Then he asked who I was. 'Morrison, eh,
a name for up ere. I knew thi father well
an t'ole surgery in Water Street.
E did is best by Earby, wi disease an that,
aye an thi mother too, deliverin bairns.
Ad thi no mind to follow in their shoes?

'Ere, ave another swig – tha's like a sheet
what started out as peachy then lost
its colourin in t'wash. Ah tell thi what:
you tek these pumps off me to elp thi ome.
They're seconds, any road, an just your size,
an tha's some sloggin still to Thornton.'

Then I was out beside him shaking hands
as he clattered off across a cattle grid,
turning left down to Elslack by the pines.
He should have come out by the Tempest
but the roak was too mawky to see beyond
the reservoir and he vanished in thin air.

That cardboard box was all I had to show
for our meeting, its pair of char-black pumps
like the ones I'd brought from school for Simon Holmes
the Christmas after his accident,
the lorry that flicked him from his bicycle
turning my mate into a sickbed ghost.

I laced the eyelets for the journey on
across the bogs and sandylands of moor.
Beside the ink-blot of a rookery
I could make out the nib of Thornton Church,
and up behind, like an act of kindness,
a perched, solitary, whitewashed farm.

And in the gorse and peat and heather-scorch
his voice came back again like judgement,
the voice of the tarns with their millstones,
a cairn of slingshot stopping me in my tracks
until the wind brought the grit of a Hargreaves
or one of the Barnoldswick MacSweens:

Get on wi thee, stuck there in t'eather
maunderin and moulderin like a corpse.
What odds would it ave made tha stayin put?
Didst think tha could cure us like thi father?
If tha'd not buggered off at twenty
tha'd as like be a boss at Silentnight,

layin us off wi no brass or future
in this valley of dead vases an mills.
So thank thi lucky stars yon ol divel's
gi'en thi some pumps to get ell out again
an shift thisen sharpish to t'nearest stickle
afore tha's eaten up by t'worms or us.

Grange Boy

Horse-chestnuts thudded to the lawn each autumn.
Their spiked husks were like medieval clubs,
porcupines, unexploded mines. But if
you waited long enough they gave themselves up –
brown pups, a cow opening its sad eye,
the shine of the dining-room table.

We were famous for horse-chestnuts. Boys
from the milltown would ring at our door asking
could they gather conkers and I'd to tell them
Only from the ground – no stick-throwing.
I watched from the casement as they wandered
in shadow, trousers crammed like mint-jars.

One morning they began without asking.
Plain as pikestaffs, their hurled sticks filleted
whole branches, the air filled like a pillowfight
with rebellion and leaves. I was alone.
I had not Father's booming voice. They were free
to trample through our peaceable estate.

Afterwards, matching Father in a show
of indignation (*bloody vandals and thugs*),
I imagined their home ground: the flagged backyards,
the forbidden ginnels and passages
winding up and out on purple moor,
the coal-sacks glistening in locked sheds.

It is June now, the chestnut scattered
like confetti. He summoned me today
to the billiard-room – that incident
with an apprentice. *I've told you before.*
A son in your father's firm, you're looked to
for an example. I don't know what to do.

So I sit at my rosewood desk, lines fading
across the parkland. I've been getting pamphlets
in a plain brown envelope and feel like
a traitor. Strangers have been seen
by the wicket-gate. Mother keeps to her bed.
English, we hoard our secrets to the end.

Metamorphoses of Childhood

I

With my pair of Labradors I lay
like Romulus under the kitchen table.

We'll be back at six, my parents would say,
abandoning me to the wolf-toothed nanny.

High above me her hands were baking
on a floured, unreachable shelf.

Later came squabbles with my fat twin-sister:
I was the handier, it seemed,

and to prove it constructed in days
a bakelite replica of Burnley.

II

The train runs right through the middle of the house...
Well, almost: they were the giants in our hedge,

breathing fire from their sooty toppers,
the burdens of the world on their back.

They were fetching for magnates:
coal, cotton, shearings of quarry.

Cars queued up to hear them at the crossing.
Our teacups trembled on tenterhooks.

I pined for release from the attic room
where a slip of the tongue had confined me.

III

Misery had no bedtime: it fell
like lead in the middle of the night.

Boum, boum, boum, boum – it was the sound
of boredom in my bloodstream,

the high room coming and going.
Why would the cornices never stay still?

First I was an elephant,
then a pin in the infinite spaces.

Marapa, marapa, I'd cry,
but my parents never heard me.

IV

Where there's muck, there's brass they said,
As in the coppery shine of cow-pats.

But then I discovered the salt-lick,
a blue whetstone lighting up the fields.

I'd been reading Scott Fitzgerald's
'The Diamond as Big as the Ritz'

and carried it home like a pools-win,
a sapphire from the mud. When I learnt the truth

it shrank in my grasp like an ice-pack:
I wept to be a prisoner of fact.

v

Death sauntered in adjoining rooms,
familiar and airy as linen.

It was the dent in Grandpa's chair,
his saying *night-night* and never returning.

Heaven must be nice: his coffin
looked plusher than a chocolate box.

And hell was just a nettle-sting
or scorch from fireworks – only ages to heal.

Why, then, Daddy's tear, lying like a lens
on my new pointy-black shoes?

A Provincial Fiction

These fields are pale with the myth
of faithless sons gone south
to the 'airs and graces of the city'.

All's lost through the loss of them:
hands dwindle at the farm
and the woods are a sighing of chainsaws.

Doctor says there's little hope.
Will you be coming up?
We've kept your room just as it always was.

The stone fires, the piebald hide
of hillsides under broken cloud,
these grounds they had and will not go back on.

Back

A griming of snow along the moortops,
water-beads sissing across the Aga,
sunlight wading through a summer-colt,
the lawn slaphappy after a shower:

before I know it I've descended to this,
a stone rectory lording it in the Pennines,
ringed by horse-chestnuts and a rookery,
near the flush Leeds-Liverpool canal.

You can drop the accent but you never lose
the slang of memory – for belled foxdocks,
the swint-ways chittering of swallows,
the lovely dung-reek of Betty Metcalf's dress.

A long shiver down the back of the land:
even in June it has that chilliness,
wind stevening over the switchbacks,
the water-meadows ruffled then glossy

like the fur down a labrador's spine.
From a far city I keep that place on
for my dream-life, a home to home in on
when I'm asleep or at the brow of it,

heart racing like our drophead Triumph
when we took the canal bridge at West Marton,
its whitewalled tyres as we hit the humpback
treading air for a moment like young lambs.

Shed Load

Like a white drinks tray carried high above the hats
of wedding guests, a hand splayed wide to balance it,
this batch of cow-parsley held itself aloof all summer

but in a week of rain has laid its head down
with the flattened wheat-stems which – puce, sodden –
sprawl in the troughs between freak-swelling waves.

Enough, enough plead the hipless sycamores,
tears running down their wrists, like children
wanting to be hugged and got back on their feet again.

Down the swept coast bedraggled picnics move inside,
a sly porthole cleared in the mist of a windscreen
bringing us this family and news about fish and chips.

And there's nothing to do but watch the valleys shaded out,
the blown diagonals like a toddler with a crayon
leaving tracks through a sketchbook's every page.

The whole country shelters in a blackout
where summer should have been, the great stormclouds
with their flares and megaphones keeping us within,

their heavy convoy rumbling in escort through lacy hedgerows
which shiver, bow and curtsy at the passing show
of armoury, the wodge of depression,

which moves inside us as we scan the horizon
for a lit crack, a resting-point, a break between lines
or carriages, a stop-off for the driven soul.

Cuckoo-pint

A brown matchstick held up in the wind,
the bract-leaf cupped around it like a palm.

March had not extinguished it: there it lurked,
sly as something done behind the sheds,

slithering from its half-unrolled umbrella
as we snipped pussy-willow from the lanes.

To come instead on this old man of the woods,
tanned and cowled and clammed inside his collar,

his shirt-front splattered with tobacco stains,
his poker oozy with tuber-froth,

was like learning by accident a secret
intended for later, exciting

and obscene and not to be gone back on,
like the knowledge of atoms, or death.

Isabella's Song

I do hate him – I am wretched – I have been a fool.
Beware of uttering one breath of this to anyone at the Grange.
                    Wuthering Heights

As I stepped out one summer night
to feed my white ring-dove
a shadow fell across the gate
and swore undying love.

The shadow stretched out tall and slim,
its face was black as night.
It spoke to me of wedding-rings
and bridesmaids bathed in light.

I left my ring-dove's pretty cote
and took that shadow's hand
and let it touch my petticoat
and ease my belly-band.

Its fingers felt as light as air.
It called me its sweet belle.
But when it lay on top of me
it crushed me like a shell.

Now I'm a shadow of myself.
I bear that shadow's bairn.
I'm running off down London way
to hide my body's shame.

So don't step out one summer night
and leave your white ring-dove.
A shadow fades as sunlight does.
Don't trust a shadow's love.

Meningococcus

'My son has gone under the hill.
We called him after a clockmaker
but God meets all such whimsy
with his early-striking hands.

That night of his high fever
I held a stream against me,
his heart panicky as a netted bird,
globes of solder on his brow.

Then he was lost in sea-fret,
the other side of silence,
his eyes milky as snowberries
and his fifteen months unlearned.

They have taken him away
who was just coming to me,
his spine like the curve
of an avocet's bill.'

Up on the Hill
after Rückert and Mahler

I

I often think: they're out walking, that's all.
Any minute they'll be back.
It's a lovely day. Relax.
Listen hard and you'll hear their cries.

Pipe down. They're out walking.
And if they've wandered
further than usual, up the hill,
we'll soon catch up with them.

They've run ahead, that's all.
When the sun's out on the hill,
we can catch up with them.
Listen hard and you'll hear their cries.

It's a lovely day, up on the hill.

II

I'd never have let them out in the wind and rain like this.
I was not consulted when they went.
No one thought to warn me what I'd feel.

I'd never have let them out in the wind and rain,
in case they caught a chill or worse.
No worse is going to happen now.

I'd have never let them out.
But the matter was taken from my hands.
They were only my children, see.

At least they're senseless now.
When lightning splits the sky,
and thunder breaks over their heads,
they lie immune,
at peace in the storm's dark eye,
at rest in their mother's home.

Gisburne Park

Originally dating from 1724, this former country home of the Lords Ribblesdale opened as a hospital in 1985. Its location overlooking acres of wooded parkland means that the finest standards of care are complemented by the restful attractions of a rural environment.

The thin-ribbed pillars in the entrance-hall
are the ones you came through for the Hunt Ball.

Beyond Reception and the waiting wheelchairs
was where you drank champagne by marble sculptures

or at the long white table helped yourself
to salmon, Aylesbury duckling or roast beef.

The talk was horsey: point-to-point, livery,
who was riding who. You shut up and ate the pureé,

knowing, after port and coffee, you'd pass out
into the floodlit garden, to waltz and foxtrot

where a band played in the sagging, striped marquee.
Today there's just a lawn, six hoops in it for croquet,

rusting now, as if the spirit had slipped through
them of the place and the era - and of you.

But the floor upstairs, where you queued in Fifties dresses
for the Ladies, is crowded still, with nurses

at their stations to direct me to the room
where you lie, worn and nametagged, like a pilgrim

at journey's end. I hold your hand as I held it
then, seeing you dressed and powdered to go out,

a child, beside myself, unable to stop, again
and again pleading for you to stay – and again,

now, despite myself, by your bed, pleading the same.

Part Three

The Ballad of the Yorkshire Ripper

The 'Red Death' had long devastated the country. No pestilence had ever been so fatal, or so hideous. Blood was its Avatar and its seal'
       Edgar Allan Poe, 'The Masque of the Red Death'

I were just cleaning up streets, our kid. Just cleaning up streets.
       Peter Sutcliffe to his brother Carl in *Somebody's*
       Husband, Somebody's Son by Gordon Burn

Ower t'ills o Bingley
stormclouds clap an drain,
like opened blood-black blisters
leakin pus an pain.

Ail teems down like stair-rods,
an swells canals an becks,
an fills up studmarked goalmouths,
an bursts on mind like sex.

Cos sex is like a stormclap,
a swellin in thi cells,
when lightnin arrers through thi
an tha knows there in't owt else.

Ah've felt it in misen, like,
ikin ome part-fresh
ower limestone outcrops
like knuckles white through flesh:

ow men clap down on women
t'old em there for good
an soak up all their softness
an lounder em wi blood.

It's then I think on t'Ripper
an what e did an why,
an ow mi mates ate women,
an ow Pete med em die.

I love em for misen, like,
their skimmerin lips an eyes,
their ankles light as jinnyspins,
their seggy whisps an sighs,

their braided locks like catkins,
an t'curlies glashy black,
the peepin o their linnet tongues,
their way o cheekin back.

An ah look on em as kindred.
But mates all say they're not,
that men must have t'owerance
or world will go to rot.

Lad-loupin molls an gadabouts,
fellow-fond an sly,
flappy-skets an drabbletails
oo'll bleed a bloke bone-dry:

that's ow I ear em spoke of
when lads are on their tod,
an ow tha's got to leather em
to stop em gi'in t'nod.

An some o t'same in Bible
where Paul screams fit to bust
ow men are fallen creatures
but womenfolk are wust.

Now I reckon this fired Peter,
an men-talk were is goad,
an culprit were our belderin God
an is ancient, bullyin road.

No, Pete weren't drove by vengeance,
rountwistedness or ale,
but to show isen a baufy man -
but let me tell thi tale.

Peter worked in a graveyard,
diggin bone and sod.
From t'grave of a Pole, Zapolski,
e eard - e reckoned - God,

sayin: 'Lad, tha's on a mission,
ah've picked thi out o t'ruck.
Go an rip up prostitutes.
They're nobbut worms an muck.

'Streets are runnin sewers.
Streets are open sores.
Get in there wi thi scalpel
an wipe away all t'oors.'

Pete were pumped like a primus.
E felt is cravin whet.
E started cruising Chapeltown
but e didn't kill, not yet.

E took a job on t'lorries,
a Transcontinental Ford.
E felt reet good in t'cabin.
E felt like a bloody Lord.

E'd bin a bit of a mardy,
angin on t'old dear's skirt.
E didn't like folks shoutin,
or scraps wi lads, or dirt.

E'd watch his dad trough offal -
trotters, liver, tripe -
or pigeon scraped from t'by-pass,
or rabbit, ung an ripe,

an all e'd felt were babbyish,
a fustilugs, alf-nowt,
an wished e were is younger kid
tekkin lasses out.

But now e'd started truckin
an ropin up is load
an brought isen a Bullworker
an swelled up like a toad,

an stuck is ead in motors
an messed wi carbs an ubs,
an drove wi mates to Manningham
an other arse-end pubs,

or sometimes off to Blackpool
to t'Tower or lights or pier,
or waxworks Chamber of Orrors -
aye, Pete were allus theer.

E met a lass called Sonia,
a nervy type, a shrew,
oo mithered im an nattered,
but Pete, e thought she'd do.

She seemed a cut above im,
a teacher, arty too,
oo wanted summat more'n kids.
Aye, Pete, e thought she'd do.

Cos Sonia, she weren't mucky,
not like yon other bags,
them tarts in fishnet stockins,
them goers, buers, slags.

～

Voice said 'Lad, get crackin:
ah've med thi bombardier.'
Pete blasted red-light districts,
eight lasses in two year.

E slit em up on wasteground,
in ginnel, plot an park,
in cemetery an woodyard,
an allus after dark.

Is tools were ball-pein ammers,
acksaws an carvin knives,
an a rusty Phillips screwdriver
oned for endin lives.

Cops dint fuss wi fust three,
paid to out on street,
though e blunted blade on is Stanley
deguttin em like meat.

Nor minded marks on fourth lass,
ripped up in her flat,
wi both ends on a clawammer,
split-splat, split-splat, split-splat.

But Jayne MacDonald were a shopgirl
sellin nobbut shoes.
Pete, e killed er anyway
an now e were front-page noos.

They appointed a Special Detective,
George Oldfield e were called.
E looked like a country bumpkin,
puffin, red, alf-bald.

E fixed up a Ripper Freefone,
Leeds 5050,
an asked Joe Soap to ring im up
an 'Tell us what you know.'

An folks, they give im names all right:
cousins, neighbours, mates,
blokes what they didn't tek to -
all were candidates.

But Pete, no e weren't rumbled.
E moved to a slap-up ouse,
pebbledash an wi a garden,
an utch to keep is mouse.

Cos Sonia, though she nittered
an med im giddyup,
were potterin too long in t'attic
to mind that owt were up.

An she went so ard at paintin
an scrubbin on ands an knee
she nivver noticed blood on trews
an t'missin cutlery.

⁓

Two weeks afore they'd folks roun
to drink to movin in
Pete ad topped another lass
an not a soul ad sin.

Now, after tekkin guests ome,
e went to t'mouldy corpse
an slashed it wi a glass pane
an serrated neck wi saws.

E were a one-man abattoir.
E cleavered girls in alves.
E shishkebab'd their pupils.
E bled em dry like calves.

Their napes as soft as foxglove,
the lovely finch-pink pout,
the feather-fern o t'eyelash -
e turned it all to nowt.

Seventh lass e totted
were in Garrads Timberyard.
E posted corpse in a pinestack
like Satan's visitin card.

Eighth were a badly woman
oo'd just come off o t'ward
o Manchester Royal Infirmary
an went back stiff as board.

E id is next on a wastetip
under a sofa's wings.
E stuffed her mouth wi ossair.
Er guts poked through like springs.

An wee Jo Whitaker, just 19,
an Alifax Buildin clerk,
bled from er smashed-egg foread
till t'gutter ran sump-dark.

There were lorry-oil inside er,
an filins in each pore,
which might ave led to Peter
if police ad looked some more.

But Oldfield, e weren't tryin.
E'd ears for nobbut 'Jack':
some oaxer wi a cassette tape
ad sent im reet off track.

Voice on tape were a Geordie's,
a tauntin, growlin loon:
'They nivver learn, George, do they.
Nice chattin. See you soon.'

George fell line an sinker,
a fishhook in is pride:
'E thinks e's cock o t'midden
but I'll see that Jack inside.'

Aye, George e took it personal,
a stand-up, man to man,
like a pair o stags wi horns locked
but Ripper offed an ran,

an wi George left fightin boggarts
e struck again like bleach:
bang in t'middle o Bradford
e wiped out Barbara Leach.

Then Marguerite Walls in Farsley,
strangled wi a noose
(a change from t'usual colander job,
none o t'normal clues).

∼

Everyweer in Yorkshire
were a creepin fear an thrill.
At Elland Road fans chanted
'Ripper 12 Police Nil.'

Lasses took up karate,
judo an self-defence,
an jeered at lads in porn shops,
an scrawled stuff in pub Gents,

like: 'Ripper's not a psychopath
but every man in pants.
All you blokes would kill like him
given half the chance.

'Listen to your beer-talk -
'hammer', 'poke' and 'screw',
'bang' and 'score' and 'lay' us:
that's what the Ripper does too.'

Aye, e did it again one last time,
to a student, Jacqueline Hill,
in a busy road, wi streetlights,
in a way more twisted still,

blammin er wi is Phillips -
but rest o that ah'll leave,
out o respect to t'family
an cos it meks me eave.

Now cops stepped up on pressure.
George, e got is cards.
Files were took from is ands
an put in Scotland Yard's.

They talked to blokes on lorries
an called at Pete's ouse twice,
but Sonia allus elped im out
wi rock-ard alibis.

It were fluke what finally nabbed im.
E'd parked is car in t'gates
of a private drive in Sheffield
wi ripped-off numberplates.

Lass oo e'd got wi im
were known to work this patch.
Cops took em both to t'station
but adn't twigged yet, natch.

Ad e meant to kill er?
E'd brought an ammer an knife
but maundered on alf evening
ow e cunt stand sight o t'wife.

Then lass passed im a rubber
an come on all coquettish.
But still e didn't touch er.
It were like a sort o death-wish.

E managed to ide is tackle
sayin e wanted a pee.
But later on is ammer
were found by a young PC.

So cops they lobbed im questions
through breakfast, dinner, tea,
till e said: 'All right, you've cracked it.
Ripper, aye, it's me.

'Ah did them thirteen killins.
Them girls live in mi brain,
mindin me o mi evil.
But ah'd do it all again.

'Streets are runnin sewers.
Streets are open sores.
Ah went there wi mi armoury
to wipe away all t'oors.

'Ah were carryin out God's mission.
Ah were following is commands.
E pumped me like a primus.
Ah were putty in is ands.'

∼

This were nub o t'court case:
were Peter reet or mad?
If lawyer could prove im a nutter
e'd not come off as bad.

Were e bats as a bizzum
or t'devil come from ell?
Choice were life in a mental
or a Parkhurst prison cell.

E sat in dock like a gipsy
wi is open sky-blue shirt
an gawped at judge an jury
as if all t'lot were dirt.

Defence called up their experts,
psychiatrists an such,
oo sed Pete weren't no sadist
an didn't rate sex much,

that e'd suffered paranoia,
allucinations too,
an killed cos is mind ad drove im -
so t'gravestone tale were true.

But t'other lot med mincemeat
o those who'd bin Pete's dupe
showin ow e'd outflanked em
to get isen from t'soup.

Cos why, if e were loopy,
ad e allus killed on t'dot,
Friday nights an Saturdays,
in cold blood not in ot?

An why, if e weren't no sadist,
ad e left girls, more 'n once,
wi a hundred stabs in t'breastbone
an planks shoved up their cunts?

An ad he shown repentance
for 't'lasses' or for 't'oors'?
As for t'religious mission:
e'd med it up, of course.

(All through this Pete's bearin
were cold as a marble slab,
ard as a joint from t'freezer,
slant as a Scarborough crab.)

Counsels rested cases.
Jury reasoned it through.
Judge said: 'How do you find him?'
'Guilty - ten to two.'

They oicked im off in a wagon
past lynchers urlin abuse
an placards urgin t'government
BRING BACK CAT AND NOOSE.

They took im to Parkhurst Prison
to serve is time an more,
an folks said t'other inmates
would know to settle t'score.

But when is face were taloned
wi a broken coffee jar
it weren't for rippin real flesh
but nudes from t'prison Star.

An meanwhile rest o t'Sutcliffes
spent up their Fleet Street brass,
an put the boot in Sonia:
'Job's all down to t'lass.

'Our Pete were nivver a nutter.
E'd allus a smile on t'face.
That Sonia nagged im rotten
till e killed oors in er place.

'Cos that's the rub wi women,
they push us blokes too far
till us can't be eld responsible
for bein what us are.'

∼

So tha sees, nowt's really altered
though Peter's out o t'way.
Mi mates still booze an charnel.
Weather's same each day.

Ower t'ills up northways
stormclouds thump an drain
like opened blood-black blisters
leakin pus an pain.

An death is like a stormclap,
a frizzlin o thi cells,
a pitchfork through thi arteries,
an tha knows there in't owt else.

It meks me think on Peter,
an what e did an why,
an ow mi mates ate women,
an ow Pete med em die.

Ah love em for misen, like,
their skimmerin lips an eyes,
their ankles light as jinnyspins,
their seggy whisps an sighs,

tiny tarn o t'navel,
chinabowl o t'ead,
stepping cairns o t'backbone,
an all e left for dead.

An I look on em as kindred.
But mates all say they're not,
that men must ave t'owerance
or world will go to rot.

An Pete were nobbut a laikin
o this belderin, umped-up God,
an served is words an logic
to rivet girls to t'sod.